ISBN:1515345106
ISBN-13:9781515345107

DEDICATION

To My wife, for allowing me to try the impossible, to see if it is possible.

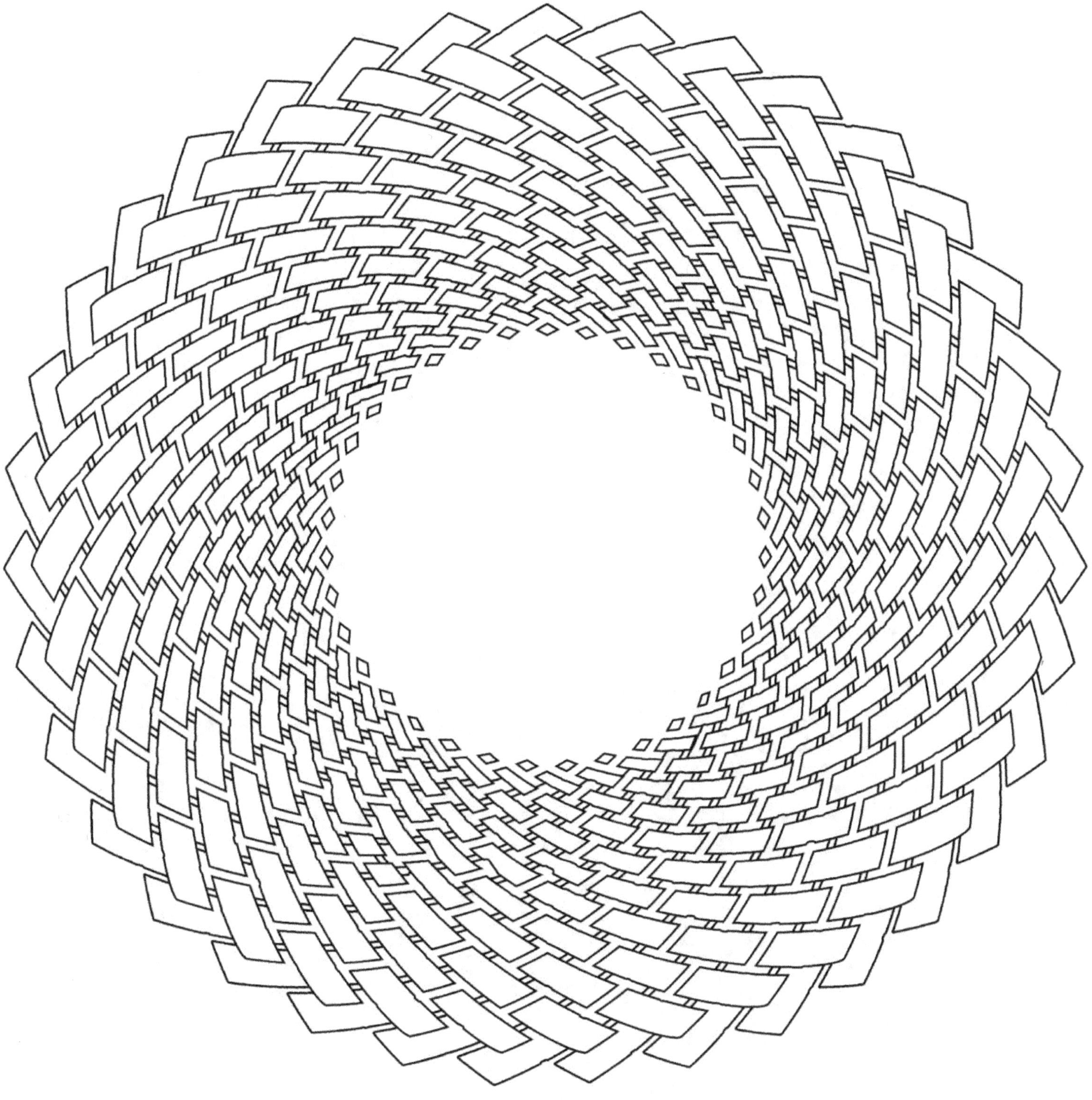

www.ingramcontent.com/pod-product-compliance
Lightning Source LLC
Chambersburg PA
CBHW080448290526
45791CB00008BA/2645